The GOLD RUSH

by Lakshmi Patel

 HOUGHTON MIFFLIN   BOSTON

A watercolor of Sutter's fort

Finding Gold

Most people in the United States knew little about California in the 1840s. Soon that would change.

The change started with John Sutter. Sutter was a wealthy landowner in California. He wanted to build a sawmill, so he hired a carpenter named James Marshall. Marshall began working on the mill. It was on the bank of the American River.

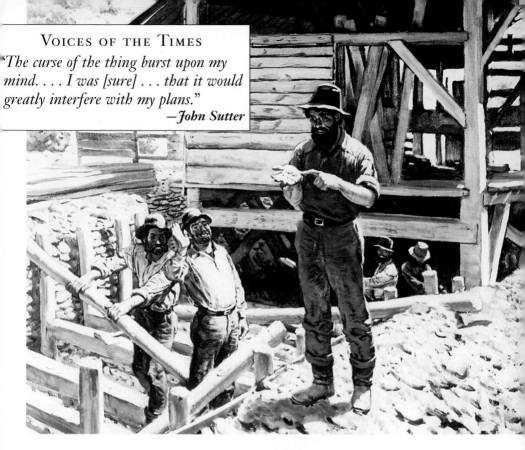

John Marshall in front of Sutter's Mill, 1852

One day, Marshall saw something shiny in the water. "I reached my hand down and picked it up," he said. "It made my heart thump." Marshall had found gold. It was January 1848.

Marshall brought the gold to Sutter, but Sutter was not happy. He knew how much the discovery of gold would change California.

Sam Brannan

When Sam Brannan heard about Marshall's find, he did not go looking for gold. He came up with another way to make money. Brannan owned a general store near Sutter's mill. First he bought mining supplies for his store. Then he took some gold dust and put it in a bottle. He went to San Francisco and walked down the streets. He shouted, "Gold! Gold! Gold from the American River!"

That was all it took. Hundreds of people left San Francisco. They came to Sutter's land, hoping to strike it rich. When they got there, they found out they needed mining supplies. Guess who they bought them from— Sam Brannan!

A painting by Victor Seaman of a miner striking it rich

Getting to California

By 1849, thousands of people had gold fever. These people were called forty-niners. They came from all over the world. They came from countries like China, Mexico, and South America. However, most came from other parts of the United States. To get to California, they came by three routes: (1) over land, (2) around the tip of South America, or (3) through the Panama Canal.

These miners came from China across the Pacific Ocean to California.

Three Routes to California

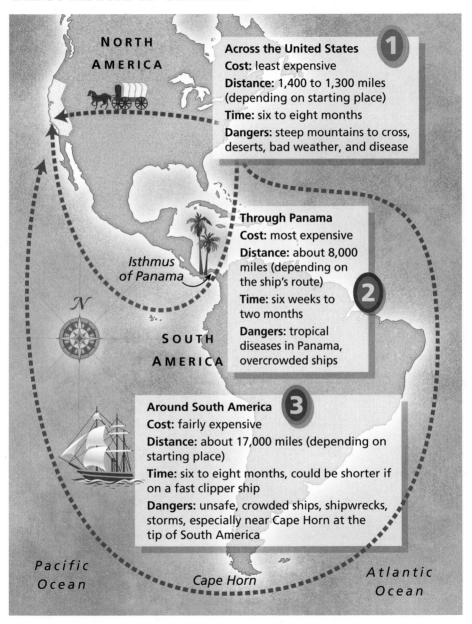

NORTH AMERICA

Across the United States ①
Cost: least expensive
Distance: 1,400 to 1,300 miles (depending on starting place)
Time: six to eight months
Dangers: steep mountains to cross, deserts, bad weather, and disease

Isthmus of Panama

Through Panama
Cost: most expensive
Distance: about 8,000 miles (depending on the ship's route)
Time: six weeks to two months
Dangers: tropical diseases in Panama, overcrowded ships ②

SOUTH AMERICA

Around South America ③
Cost: fairly expensive
Distance: about 17,000 miles (depending on starting place)
Time: six to eight months, could be shorter if on a fast clipper ship
Dangers: unsafe, crowded ships, shipwrecks, storms, especially near Cape Horn at the tip of South America

N

Pacific Ocean

Cape Horn

Atlantic Ocean

At the Diggings

Forty-niners dug for gold near rivers. They searched through sand and dirt. They hoped to find gold dust, flakes, or gold nuggets (lumps of gold). Many of the miners had never worked so hard before.

Miners used many different kinds of equipment to find gold.

Alvin Coffey used the money he earned from mining to buy his freedom.

Mining camps were rough places. Most roads were dirt paths. Miners lived in huts. Food and clothing were scarce. Camps were dirty and poor, so many miners became ill. In fact, one miner out of five died from disease. In addition, there were few law officers. Arguments between miners often ended in violence.

Alvin Coffey had a hard life in the mines, but he earned something better than gold from his time in California—his freedom. He was enslaved when he arrived. He bought his freedom with money he earned mining.

We Were Here First

The gold rush was hard on the people who already lived in California. Many California Indians were pushed off their land. They were forced to work for miners. The miners treated them like slaves. Others were killed by miners, but the miners were not punished.

These California Indians were forced to leave their lands and make a home in Yosemite.

A Californio family

Spanish-speaking families who lived in California when Spain and then Mexico ruled were called *Californios*. They also lost land. Before the gold rush, they had been wealthy landowners. When California became part of the United States, the U.S. had signed a treaty with Mexico. The treaty said that families in California could keep their property. Many forty-niners ignored the treaty. They staked claims on the land.

Miners crowd into a small area to look for gold.

Facing Challenges

As more and more people moved to California, it became hard to find gold. Miners tried to keep others away from their claims. They also tried to keep people out of California. In 1852, California passed a law. The law forced mine workers from other countries to pay a tax. Another law forced ships to pay a tax if they carried someone into California from another country.

By the mid-1850s, it was getting even harder to find gold. The only gold left was at the bottom of rivers or deep underground. So groups of people formed companies. They combined their money. They bought large machines that dug deep under the earth to find gold. Sometimes they made lots of money.

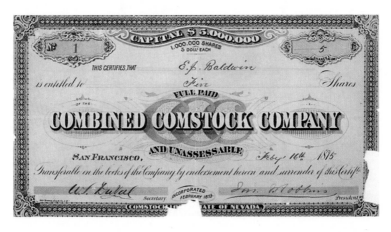

A share certificate from the Combined Comstock Company: one of the most successful mining groups of the 1850s.

13

New Businesses

Miners weren't the only ones who struck it rich. Hundreds of other people made money. They were entrepreneurs, or people with their own businesses. They provided the miners with food, clothing, and hotel rooms. Sometimes, after a few hard months, the miners gave up mining. They learned they could make money other ways. They became storekeepers, carpenters, lawyers, or doctors.

Mifflin Gibbs was one of the owners of the Pioneer Boot and Shoe Emporium.

Employees of Levi Strauss and Company in San Francisco, around 1880

Levi Strauss made money on miners. He came to the U.S. from Bavaria in 1835. He sold sturdy cloth to tailors in San Francisco. The tailors used the cloth to make pants for miners. Later, his company made pants with metal rivets (small rods). These pants would become the jeans that are still worn today.

San Francisco in 1878

After the Gold Rush

The gold rush did not last long. But it affected people's attitudes about California. Thousands of Americans thought of California as a place where they could make a lot of money. They thought it was a place where they could start their lives over again. People still think of the state that way. Many call it the "land of opportunity."